SHORT PRAYER

GREG MITCHELL

To Matt McPhee
—the St Anthony of my soul

Copyright © 1995 Greg Mitchell

The author asserts the moral right
to be identified as the author of this work

First published in Australia in 1995 by
Dove, an imprint of HarperCollins*Publishers* (Australia) Pty Ltd
First published in the UK in 1997 by
Lion Publishing plc
Sandy Lane West, Oxford, England
ISBN 0 7459 3821 3

First edition 1997
10 9 8 7 6 5 4 3 2 1 0

A catalogue record for this book is available from the British Library

Designed by William Hung
Cover design by William Hung
Cover illustration by Kim Roberts, based on an illustration concept by Greg Mitchell
Illustrations by Kim Roberts, based on illustration concepts by Greg Mitchell
Printed and bound in Malta by Interprint

ON BEING A PRAYER PRAY-ER

When I pray I ask a lot of questions . . .

Dear God, Do you ever get sick of all of my questions? Amen.

I'm not usually a good prayer pray-er.

Dear God, Why do I always look so good when I appear to be praying but I'm really thinking of food? Amen.

The prayers presented here tend to arrive in my mind whole and complete.

Dear God, How come jokes often come with sharp edges? Amen.

They are whimsical but carry with them real truths.

Dear God, Can you pray without knowing that you're doing it? Amen.

They are often challenging and sometimes baffling.

Dear God, Are there atheists in heaven? Amen.

But they make you feel that it's always good to have someone to talk to.

Dear God, When is the best time for me to call? Amen.

D E A R GOD

I come to pray …

that I pray well.

Amen

DEAR GOD

Help me to be

a thin person ...

with a fat heart.

Amen

DEAR GOD

Put me to the test ...

but don't let me know

the score.

Amen

DEAR GOD

Help me to remember you …

before I get into trouble.

Amen

DEAR GOD

I am sitting here

waiting for you to call.

I will try desperately

to be home.

Amen

DEAR GOD

Help me appreciate the young

when I am old,

and comprehend the old

while I am young.

Amen

DEAR GOD

Open my ears,

shut my mouth,

and let my heart

do the talking.

Amen

DEAR GOD

Thank you for all the things

you have made.

You must have spent hours

on flowers.

Amen

DEAR GOD

Help me

not to be

distracted.

Amen

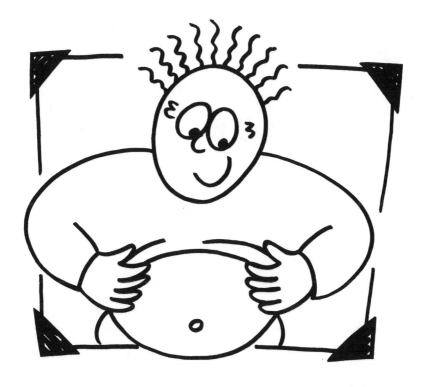

DEAR GOD

Lead me away from self pity,

so that I never fall

into my own open wounds.

Amen

DEAR GOD

Help me to see the light

and understand the heavy.

Amen

DEAR GOD

Please grease

my squeaking wheels.

Amen

DEAR GOD

Help me to love other people,

as much as I love my dog.

Amen

<u>DEAR</u> GOD

Let me only make mistakes

that don't matte~~rrr~~r.

Amen

DEAR GOD

Help me to learn that my

slow emotion replays

are not the whole picture.

Amen

DEAR GOD

Can I pray

with my hands in my pockets

and my shirt hanging out?

Amen

DEAR GOD

Help me find the child I was ...

and hug it with love.

Amen

DEAR GOD

Tell me ...

how did Mary and Joseph cope ...

when Jesus was two?

Amen

DEAR GOD

When I'm too tired to cry ...

let me laugh.

Amen

DEAR GOD

Kick me when I forget

that football is only a game.

Amen

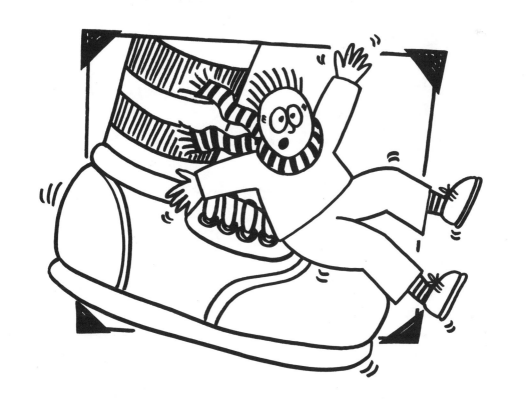

DEAR GOD

Why does prayer come easy ...

when there's something else

worse to do?

Amen

DEAR GOD

Teach me that "silent" and "listen"

are anagrams that mean prayer.

Amen

DEAR GOD

Help me to remember

that relationships are the intersections

and not just

the one-way streets.

Amen

DEAR GOD

Make me always fill up

the jug of life …

and not just drink from it …

and put it back in the fridge.

Amen

DEAR GOD

Why do fluttering candles

attract the most attention?

Amen

DEAR GOD

Let me learn

that I am blessed with fatness ...

in a world cursed by starvation.

Amen

DEAR GOD

Help me to look for things

that are the same in others,

and not what is different.

Amen

DEAR GOD

Lead me to buckets of silence …

when my mouth begins to fire.

Amen

DEAR GOD

Help me to tell the truth ...

even when it spoils

a good story.

Amen

DEAR GOD

Never let me be drunk

while I am driving my emotions.

Amen

DEAR GOD

I hope you have a thesaurus

for when I say I'm depressed.

Amen

DEAR GOD

Let my prayers be

vibrant conversations with you ...

and not a staff meeting.

Amen

DEAR GOD

Let me live

as if the world is safe …

even when I'm scared to death.

Amen

DEAR GOD

Coax my thoughts

to fly with angels ...

while my feet tap dance

firmly on the ground.

Amen

DEAR GOD

Help me swing on

all the vines …

in the jungle

of my heart.

Amen

DEAR GOD

Teach me that paperwork

is far less important

than people work.

Amen

DEAR GOD

What song

did you have in mind ...

when you made my voice?

Amen

DEAR GOD

Help me to be

a learner with insight,

rather than

an expert in hindsight.

Amen

DEAR GOD

Force me to be

as generous with my money

as I am with my advice.

Amen

DEAR GOD

Lure me to tangents

that lead me to you.

Amen

DEAR GOD

Provide me with a noble "No!"

instead of a yo-yoing "Yes!"

Amen

DEAR GOD

When you made the world,

how did you choose

the color scheme?

Amen

DEAR GOD

If I go forth,

can I come first?

Amen

DEAR GOD

Do you answer prayers

that ain't done good?

Amen

DEAR **GOD**

YAHWEH MOST HIGH
SUPERIOR BEING
SHE

Whatever your name is!
Do you know who I am?

Amen

DEAR GOD

Why is bad

so entertaining?

Amen

DEAR GOD

Remind me

that we all live

in glass houses.

Amen

DEAR GOD

What did Jesus do

at school?

Amen

DEAR GOD

May my halo

be the "hello"

I give to those I meet.

Amen

DEAR GOD

In the great

sock drawer of life,

let me be paired

with the odd people.

Amen

DEAR GOD

Lead me to pilot my future

with the truth of my past.

Amen

DEAR GOD

Do prayers have a

"use by" date?

Amen

DEAR GOD

Help me to put right

those who are left out.

Amen

DEAR GOD

If I must love my neighbor,

can I move

to another suburb first?

Amen

DEAR GOD

If you must, take me tonight ...

so that if I wake

I will know

that the day is mine.

Amen

DEAR GOD

Is meeting You

Youtopia?

Amen

DEAR GOD

I place my life

in your hands.

I hope that they are warm.

Amen

DEAR GOD

Help me to be

predictably

unpredictable.